Praying Advent

Series Preface

The volumes in NCP's "7 x 4" series offer a meditation a day for four weeks, a bite of food for thought, a reflection that lets a reader ponder the spiritual significance of each and every day. Small enough to slip into a purse or coat pocket, these books fit easily into everyday routines.

Praying Advent

Three Minute Reflections on Peace, Faithfulness, Joy, and Light

Joan Mueller

New City Press
Hyde Park, New York

Published in the United States by New City Press
202 Comforter Blvd., Hyde Park, NY 12538
www.newcitypress.com
©2010 Joan Mueller

Cover design by Durva Correia

Library of Congress Cataloging-in-Publication Data:

Mueller, Joan, 1956-
   Praying Advent : three minute reflections on peace, faithfulness, joy, and
light / Joan Mueller.
      p. cm. — ("7 x 4" : A meditation a day for four weeks)
   Includes bibliographical references.
   ISBN 978-1-56548-358-3 (pbk. : alk. paper) 1. Advent—Meditations.
   2. Devotional literature. I. Title.
   BV40.M84 2010
   242'.33—dc22   2010024306

Printed in the United States of America

Contents

one
Peace

two
Faithfulness

three
Joy

four
Light

Introduction

For many Christians, Advent is their favorite season, yet they find themselves overshadowed with shopping, preparations for Christmas, unexpected snow and ice storms, holiday parties, and endless other distractions. Although the tree might be decorated and the presents wrapped, Christmas sometimes simply falls upon us, our souls feeling woefully unprepared.

Praying Advent hopes to help prepare busy souls for the true Christmas season. The book is divided into four weeks, with a scripture reading, reflection, and spiritual practice for each day. If you cannot do a reflection on a certain day, just pick the book up the next day and begin again. The object is not perfect discipline, but to be better prepared for the Christmas season. Like a tree that is dressed with lights, garland, ornaments, and a crib below, these reflections dress our souls. While some readers' preparations will, perhaps, be more elaborate than that of others, we can imagine God smiling at a busy soul, and reveling in the beauty of its simple preparation. "The best we can do" is truly a gift that brings delight to God.

Begin by slowly reading the Advent scripture reading. You may wish to take a few minutes pondering it before reading the reflection that follows. Or you may prefer to take a minute of silence after the reflection. Following the reflection is a suggested spiritual practice that can be done during the course of the day. Feel free to adjust this rhythm according to your own needs. Find your own preference and trust that it is God's path for you.

Think of the suggested spiritual practice as a physical exercise that can be adjusted to the needs of your own body type. Try to practice it throughout the day, but if you forget just try again tomorrow.

During the fourth week, Christmas is the last reflection and may be used on Christmas day.

In Advent we celebrate both that God has already come, yet is coming. Already encircled by infinite divine life and love, we try to awaken our souls to God's vibrant presence. This month-long journey can beautify souls and awaken hearts to the presence of Emmanuel — God with us.

Peace

one

1 Leveling the Mountains and Hills

Scripture Reading: Luke 3:3–6

John preached a baptism of repentance for the forgiveness of sins, as it is written in the book of the prophet Isaiah:

> A voice cries out in the desert:
> "Prepare the way of the Lord.
> Make straight God's paths.
> Every valley shall be filled
> and every mountain and hill shall be leveled.
> Winding roads will be made straight,
> rough paths will be made smooth,
> and every human person
> shall see the salvation of God!"

Reflection

The Advent season calls us to "repent" from the busyness of our lives to the quiet, reverence, and peace necessary to welcome a baby into the world. To do this, we must make room for the child, cleaning up and simplifying our lives from unnecessary outer and inner clutter. On the outside, we are asked to level every mountain of superfluous possessions and offer them to those whose need is a valley waiting to be filled. On the inside, we are to discern what is winding and rough, straightening out our relationships as best we can and smoothing our rough personal edges.

Spiritual Practice

What in my life is superfluous and might be given to others? Can I organize just a small corner of my life and give what I do not need to someone who needs it? Perhaps today I might straighten out a cupboard, a closet, or a corner of a room.

A Spa Day for the Soul

Scripture Reading: Isaiah 2:4

They shall beat their swords into plowshares
and their spears into pruning hooks.
One nation shall not raise the sword against
    another nation;
nor shall they train for war again.

Reflection

While external clutter is rather easily cured with a big waste basket and a donation bag, internal clutter is a more difficult matter. During the holidays, relatives can sometimes seem hard-wired to cause us hardship, co-workers can more readily get on our nerves, and our stress levels can elevate completely out of control. Unlike cleaning our closets, we can't collect our stress and donate it to someone else. Our stress is our own, and we have to deal with it.

We live in a stress-filled world and can only do what we can to manage stress. We want to be constructive with our stress, "beating our swords into plowshares and our spears into pruning hooks." We want to quit "training for war" and use the energy of our stress for peace.

Spiritual Practice

Try to identify what is stressing you out. Is it a problem with a child, a neighbor, a co-worker? Is it a money matter, a situation at work, a deadline? Whatever it is, try to think of a way to "chill" the stress just for today. If stress is caused by another person, try giving yourself a little physical and emotional space from that person. If it is caused by a situation, remove yourself a bit from the situation. Measure your stress level now, and see if you can develop a strategy to "chill" your stress down at least a few degrees by this time tomorrow.

3 Guide Us on the Way of Peace

Scripture Reading: Matthew 10:12–13

When you enter a house, wish those within
   it peace.
If the house is worthy, your peace will come
   upon it.
If not, let your peace return to you.

Reflection

Stress is the symptom of a lack of peace in our lives. In the Gospel of Matthew, Jesus tells us not to make war against people and situations that cost us our peace, but merely to give thanks when our peace is received and to move on when it is not. We want to look for relationships and situations that bring us peace and foster deeper peace. We want to welcome those people and circumstances that deepen our peace rather than those that sap the life out of us.

We also want to care for our own inner "house" and bring it peace. We want to treat our soul with mercy, kindness, and sympathy, rather than be a stern master who hurts and harms. Sometimes this will demand a change in behavior, but our divinized souls should never be belittled or demeaned. We are literally the tabernacle of God. Peace lives within us. Peace is at the root of our very being.

Spiritual Practice

As you journey today, try to identify who or what brings peace into your life. Are you making the most of these opportunities and relationships? Are they your priority? Next, try to identify who or what saps your peace. Is there a way to put some space between yourself and these persons or situations? Remember, there is no need to label someone or a situation as "good" or "bad." The call is simply to try to find the path to God's peace.

4 Surrendering Our Worries to God

Scripture Reading: Philippians 4:6–7

Don't be anxious.
Rather with prayer, petition, and thanksgiving
make your needs known to God.
Then God's peace, which is beyond all
understanding,
will guard your hearts and minds in Christ
Jesus.

Reflection

We all want to be peaceful, and during the Advent season we wish to prepare our souls for the peace of Christmas. We want to welcome the child of Christmas with a peaceful spirit, not with stress and anxiety. Paul identifies anxiety as the critical adversary of peace, but anxiety is part of life. How do we deal with it?

Teresa of Avila tells us that the ultimate secret of the spiritual life is to take care of God's business on earth and then to ask God to take care of our problems. While many of us are dutiful in trying to do God's will, we fail to ask for God's help in the process. Saint Paul reminds us to hand our worries over to God with "prayer, petition, and thanksgiving."

Spiritual Exercise

Identify what is stressing you out. What do you need from God to help you with the situation? Try at least three times today to ask God for what you need to make the situation more manageable. Remember, God's deal with us is that if we do our best to do the work of God on earth, God will take care of what is beyond our control. All we have to do is offer our worries to God in prayer.

5 Becoming Mindful

Scripture Reading: Jeremiah 30:22

You shall be my people,
and I shall be your God.

Reflection

When I was young, I decided to study the whole of the Old Testament. I read a book at a time with commentaries to better understand the historical and spiritual context of the text. I remember the day that I finished: I closed my Bible and thought that the entire Old Testament can be summarized in one line — "You shall be my people, and I shall be your God."

No matter what human beings do, no matter how degenerate or unfaithful we are, God still wants to be in relationship with us. God disregards our past, our bad habits, our infidelities, and our moodiness, and does not say, "Get your life together and we'll see then if you are worthy." Rather, over and over again we are invited into divine relationship. We are made for God and, it seems, God does everything possible to be in relationship with us.

Spiritual Exercise

During the season of Advent we celebrate the mystery of God coming to us and living with us. Today, every time you see a baby or young child, try to remember how much God wants to be in love, in relationship with you.

A Peace Break

Scripture Reading: Matthew 11:28–30

If you find yourself burdened, come to me.
I will give you rest.
Take up my yoke, and learn from me,
for I am gentle and humble of heart
and you will find rest for your soul.
For my yoke is easy,
and my burden is light.

Reflection

In transitioning to the time of Advent, we find how much we struggle with our own worries and cares. We feel burdened, overwhelmed by obligations, anxiety, and deadlines.

God knows how quickly we become anxious. God knows that we must be reminded over and over again to trust, to hand over our worries, and to rest in God's peace. During this first week, we focus on trying to enter the peace of the Advent season. Peace is not a goal, however, but a process. Every day, hour, and minute we renew our desire for peace.

Spiritual Exercise

Today, try to do one thing that might bring you peace. Buy a cup of coffee and enjoy a ten-minute break. Do some shopping. Take a twenty-minute walk at lunchtime. Or have a special story time this evening with your children.

Living a
Child's Dream

Scripture Reading: Isaiah 11:6

Then the wolf will live with the lamb,
and the leopard shall lie down with the goat.
The calf and the young lion shall browse
   together,
and a little child will lead them.

Reflection

Isaiah presents us with what seems to be a surreal world. Predators and prey no longer fear each other. Instinct is subdued and wolves and leopards magically become vegetarians! This is a world unlike our own; it is the world pictured by a child. There is complete harmony because the child has not yet experienced the complexities and cares of life.

The child with this dream still lives in us even as we mature. Certainly, we are not naïve enough to expect that those interested in "eating" us will suddenly become beneficent. We can, however, work on our own "wolfness" and "leopardness" to make the child's dream more of a reality. Rather than promoting aggression, we can actively choose peace.

Spiritual Exercise

Reflect on where you might be tempted to be a "wolf" or "leopard" today. Who invites your aggression? What situations tempt you to frustration? How do you bad-mouth or "eat" the reputation of another? Within your own soul, is there a "lion" that undermines your self-esteem or self-worth?

Now, develop a strategy to permit the lion and lamb to pasture together just for today. Give a compliment to someone you would prefer to bad-mouth; do an act of kindness to someone who irritates you; comfort your own soul with kind words rather than with judgment.

Faithfulness

two

Inviting God's Indwelling Presence

Scripture Reading: Isaiah 7:14

> The Lord himself will give you this sign:
> A virgin will conceive and bear a son,
> and name him "Emmanuel."

Reflection

While we might worry sometimes that God has forsaken us, God gives us a sign. "A virgin will conceive and bear a son, and name him 'Emmanuel.'" The name, Emmanuel, we know, means "God is with us."

If God is truly with us, we know that we need not struggle through life alone. What a shame it would be for a lonely person to have a ready companion who they refuse to see, struggling through life alone when someone desperately wants to be with them. God tells us that God is with us — yesterday, today, and tomorrow.

Spiritual Exercise

Ponder today how God is present in your life. Where do you experience God's faithfulness and peace? Do you invite God's faithfulness and peace into your life, or do you continue to keep God distant?

God comes to us not as a powerful force trying to coerce us into obedience, but as an infant born in a manger. God comes to us as a baby so that we do not fear, so that we can invite the child into our arms. Today, ponder how you might embrace even more deeply God's love and care for you. Invite the love, light, and peace of God to dwell deeply into your heart.

2 Doing One Good Thing

Scripture Reading: 1 Thessalonians 5:22–24

Refrain from all evil.
May the God of peace make you holy,
and may your spirit, soul, and body
remain blameless for the coming of Jesus
    Christ.
God who calls you is faithful,
and God will accomplish this.

Reflection

Paul tells the Thessalonians to "refrain from evil." In order to develop a faithful lifestyle, we must choose the peace of Christ with fidelity. In other words, day after day we must choose the way to peace. This means not only to avoid the temptation to cause distress and conflict with others, but also to avoid, as best we can, situations that lead to distress and conflict.

Sometimes we are not blameless. Perhaps we provoke the weakness of other people or gossip in an attempt to belittle another person to our advantage. Perhaps we interpret another's intention in the worse possible way, rather than giving them the benefit of the doubt. Paul asks us to refrain from these behaviors and to present ourselves holy before God in spirit, soul, and body.

Spiritual Exercise

Try to assess situations where you might not be entirely blameless. Consider situations of conflict in your life, and how you might be at least partially to blame. Gently, knowing that only God can truly bring us salvation, think of one small way that you might bring good, either to this situation directly, or to another one, as a way to repent for any conflict you might have caused. Do one thing, and then be peaceful. God is in charge, and God is faithful.

Becoming Faithful

Scripture Reading: Romans 13:13–14

Let us conduct ourselves properly as in
   daylight,
not in orgies and drunkenness,
not in promiscuity and licentiousness,
not in rivalry and jealousy.
Rather, put on the Lord Jesus Christ,
and make no provision for the desires of the
   flesh.

Reflection

We usually behave ourselves during the day,
and, if we are prone to trouble, Paul suggests
that we tend to misbehave at night. Paul gives
us a list of behaviors that he feels are particularly
problematic for the faithful following of Jesus:
orgies, drunkenness, promiscuity, licentiousness,
rivalry, and jealousy. He does not distinguish
orgies from jealousy; promiscuity from rivalry.
Each of us has our weakness, and each of us must
faithfully work against our weakness in order to
follow Jesus.

Spiritual Exercise

Examine carefully Paul's list of problematic behaviors:

Orgies
Drunkenness
Promiscuity
Licentiousness
Rivalry
Jealously

Which behavior (choose only one for today), is most problematic for you?

Spend a minute thinking about what you might do to work against this behavior in order to become a more faithful follower of Jesus. Do you need to cancel out of a holiday party in order to avoid temptation? Might a call to Alcoholics Anonymous be helpful? Do you need to speak good words about someone you have formerly maligned? Don't be overwhelmed; just do one thing that helps you move in the direction of faithfulness. Then, trust that God will be pleased with your effort and will provide further grace.

4 Basking in God's Light

Scripture Reading: James 5:7–8

Be patient, brothers and sisters,
until the Lord comes.
See how the farmer remains patient both in
    early and late rains
waiting for the produce of his field.
You, too, must be patient.
Make your heart steadfast,
because the Lord is coming soon.

Reflection

God's grace is like a seed planted in a farmer's field. God faithfully provides the sun and the rain. It is the job of the farmer to keep the field weeded as best as possible, and to be patient. The potential for growth is within the seed itself — it is a God-given potential.

When we look at our own lives, at our own faithfulness to the spiritual journey, sometimes we feel as though we have not been too successful in overcoming our shortcomings. Even after many years, we find that we still gossip, become impatient, suffer from anxiety, or burden others with our neediness.

Our soul carries within it the seed of God's dream, God's holiness for us. God's harvest will come within us, and the miracle of the crop will reflect not only our small efforts but also the sun of God's love and the rain of God's faithfulness.

Spiritual Exercise

Reflect today on how you are impatient with your own soul. Is there a shortcoming that makes you angry with yourself? Are you frustrated with the limitations of your body or mind? Do you see yourself as deficient in any way?

Hold the reason of your impatience up to the sun of God's love and the rain of God's faithfulness. Remember that, while you might do a little weeding, it is primarily God who will bring about the miracle of holiness in your soul.

Thank God for the beauty of your soul and the beauty of the holiness God is creating within you. Perhaps repeat the prayer of Clare of Assisi: "I praise and thank you, God, for having created me!"

5 Praising God for Creating You!

Scripture Reading: Isaiah 11:1–5

A shoot will sprout from the stump of Jesse,
and from its roots a bud shall blossom.
The spirit of the Lord will rest upon him.
A spirit of wisdom and understanding,
a spirit of counsel and of strength
a spirit of knowledge and of the fear of the
    Lord.
Not by appearance shall he judge,
nor shall he make decisions through hearsay.
Rather he will judge the poor with justice,
and favor those who suffer.
Justice shall gird his waist,
and faithfulness will be a belt around his hips.

Reflection

While God appreciates our efforts to work against our weaknesses, God also has graced us with abundant strengths. Some of us are wise and can see our way through complex situations. Others understand the hearts of other people or have a sympathetic ear. Still others are able to counsel the young or the troubled. Some of us serve as a source of strength to those who count on it to give them protection. Some are astute in knowledge and have the ability to forge ahead in science, industry, or the arts. A few may have an innate reverence for God, and understand in a very natural way God's grandeur and grace.

Human beings are creatures both gifted and challenged. We are not created equally but uniquely. When God looks upon us, God sees us as we were created. God feels delicate sympathy and understanding toward us, and judges in favor of us.

Spiritual Exercise

Identify the gift that God has naturally placed within your soul:

Wisdom
Understanding
Counsel
Strength
Knowledge
Fear of the Lord.

Hold this gift up to God and thank God again for the beauty of your own soul. Again you might wish to pray Saint Clare's prayer: "I praise and thank you, God, for having created me!"

Adopted into God's Family

Scripture Reading: 1 Corinthians 1:8–9

Jesus will keep you faithful until the end,
so that you will be blameless on the day of
Jesus Christ.
God is faithful,
and has called you into communion
with his Son, Jesus Christ our Lord.

Reflection

Unless we undermine God's ability to delight
in the beauty of our souls by clinging to anxiety,
God's fidelity guarantees that the seed of holiness
will grow and mature in us. Anxiety is our way
of pretending that we are God. If we faithfully
choose the path of peace by actively discerning
where we can most profitably make a difference,
and by avoiding situations that sap our time and
energy to little avail, then the seed of goodness in
us will naturally grow in the light of God's love
and faithfulness.

Jesus Christ is in communion with the Father
and the Spirit. The Trinity of God is held together
by the dynamic love they have for each other.

Through Jesus Christ, we have been made adopted sons and daughters of God. This means that each of us are actually made members of the family of God — the Trinity. We are invited into Trinitarian union not because we are perfect but because we are baptized. To experience the dynamism and gift of this Trinitarian union, we simply need to let go of our anxiety and trust in God's faithfulness.

Spiritual Exercise

Picture, as you are able, the love between Father, Son, and Spirit. Remembering that through your baptism you have been adopted into the Trinitarian family, picture yourself included within this family of God.

7 Being Christ's Hands in Our World

Scripture Reading: Luke 1:38

Mary said,
"Behold, I am the servant of the Lord.
Let it be done to me according to your
    word."

Reflection

To be faithful to God, we simply need to pray
Mary's prayer: "I am the servant of the Lord. Let it
be done to me according to your word." Our role
as God's human creatures is not to make ourselves God, but to be the hands, feet, and heart
of God in the world. When we are worried or
upset, we need to hand these cares to God, since
by doing so, we admit that we are not God.

Yet, there are times when God needs us.
Because God is spirit, God must love the world
through creatures — through us. When God
needed Mary's help, Mary offered herself. Without us, God cannot bring the neighbor cookies,
bring the sorrowing dinner, teach a child to read,
or practice prayers with the grandchildren.

Spiritual Exercise

What are your worries? Let God know what you need today.

Now listen to what God needs from you today. What are the needs of your family, friends, neighbors, or co-workers today? What is it possible for you to peacefully accomplish?

God is faithful. Do your best today to be God's hands and feet in the world, and trust that God will take care of your worries. Let God be God, and be content to do your part as a creature by offering to bring just a little of God's love and joy into the world this day.

Joy

Planting Random Acts of Kindness

Scripture Reading: Philippians 4:4–5

Rejoice always in the Lord.
I say it again, rejoice!
Let your kindness be evident to all.
The Lord is near.

Reflection

What does it mean to rejoice in the Lord? St. Paul tells us that joy is connected to our kindness. We are to be kind and this kindness should be evident to all. Evident kindness is the sign, for Paul, that the Lord is truly near.

This doesn't mean that we are to go through the world publicizing our every kind deed, but that we do the best we can to speak a kind word of truthful encouragement or do a thoughtful deed when given the opportunity. Most likely Paul would have liked the idea of "random acts of kindness." Surprising others with kindness is like a boomerang — it comes back to us.

Spiritual Exercise

Joy is a choice. Ask yourself: Where could I be more joyful in my life? Why am I not as joyful as I could be?

Paul's suggestion for increasing our joy is to spread "random acts of kindness." Who in my life could use a kind word or deed? Cultivate a few seeds of kindness today and ask the Holy Spirit to water and warm these seeds. Keep planting "random acts of kindness," pray, and wait, knowing that the Lord will take our small gifts and bless them one-hundredfold.

2 Giving Joy

Scripture Reading: Luke 1:43–45

Elizabeth cried out in a loud voice and said:
"How does it happen that the mother of my
   Lord should come to me?
For as soon as I heard your greeting,
the baby in my womb leaped for joy.
Blessed is she who believed that what was
   spoken to her by the Lord
would be fulfilled."

Reflection

Elizabeth was a woman beyond childbearing years during an age when birthing a child, even when one was young, was a very dangerous undertaking. As her time came near, she must have been quite nervous. As an older woman, she should have been *acting* as a midwife, not looking for one!

We know what it's like to feel alone when we need the help of someone kind. How frightening it is to go to the hospital for surgery when we are alone at home without anyone to help us recover. How lonely it is to celebrate a personal event without our friends nearby. How difficult it is to travel and return without someone to welcome us home.

One can understand why Elizabeth felt such joy when she saw her cousin, Mary. Even the baby within her womb recognized Elizabeth's relief and jumped for joy. We need each other's tenderness in order to be human, joyful people.

Spiritual Exercise

Who might you bring joy to today? Who depends upon your kindness and tenderness? If possible, call or e-mail that person today and wish him or her well. Does a neighbor need a meal today? Does a child need a gift? Rather than looking for a charity to donate to, give a gift to someone who would find real joy in a gesture that comes from you. Does someone you love need to be forgiven? Does a neighbor need a kind word? Today would be the day to bring this joy to another's heart.

3 Gifting the Burden

Scripture Reading: Zechariah 2:14–15

Sing for joy, O daughter Zion!
See, I am coming to live among you, says
   the Lord.
Many nations will join the Lord on that day.
You shall become God's people,
and God will dwell among you.

Reflection

Imagine how joyful life might be if we could simply place our anxieties in God's hands knowing with confidence that God would take care of us. Yet, how does God take care of us if not through the kindness of others? As Christians we are called to act kindly and tenderly in our world, and this very kindness invites the presence of God among us.

Many times, those with the most worries and cares are those who do not have adequate resources to feel safe in this world. A mother must choose to buy a Christmas gift or to pay the heating bill, or a father would buy his wife something special, but the mortgage eats his entire paycheck.

Spiritual Exercise

Examine today how you might be connected to someone who has a true need. Is there someone in your church — a refugee family, a family who has encountered a tragedy or is burdened with a health crisis — who needs God's love today?

If so, contemplate whether it may be possible for you to gift the burden rather than the joy. If a parent cannot buy a gift because the rent is a burden, offer to pay the rent so that the parent can have the joy of buying a Christmas gift for their own child. Perhaps a little time off might offer a caretaker the possibility of providing a more beautiful and tender Christmas for their loved one. What can you do to notice the truly needy in your life today?

Flowers in the Desert

Scripture Reading: Isaiah 35:1–2

The desert and the parched land will exult.
The steppe will rejoice and blossom.
It will bloom with flowering abundance,
and exult with joyful song.
The glory of Lebanon will be given to them,
the splendor of Carmel and Sharon.
They will see the glory of the Lord,
the splendor of our God.

Reflection

True peace happens not when we barricade ourselves behind steel fences, but when we see the needs of those who are truly desperate living among us. They are the desert and the parched land. Perhaps they live across town where we are careful not to go. Perhaps they are integrated into our neighborhood. Whatever the case, the parched land exists and needs irrigation to thrive.

A flowering desert is a beautiful thing. The miracle of colors in a land ridden with drought and precariousness brings joy to even the coldest heart. This is the miracle God wishes to create today.

Spiritual Exercise

Who are the desperately poor in your community and who is connected to them? Is there an organization that gives direct aid to those who are close to desperation? Does your church have a ministry to those who need food, clothing, or shelter? Does a food pantry or homeless shelter need assistance? Does a refugee family in your neighborhood need rice, vegetables, and fruit?

Mary and Joseph depended upon the kindness of others in order to bring Jesus into the world. They were greeted by the shepherds and those who were wealthy — the three kings. Whether shepherds or kings, we have a gift for those who are in desperate need. What gift might I give the truly desperate today?

5 Accepting the Hundredfold

Scripture Reading: Luke 1:46–49

Mary said,
"My soul proclaims the greatness of the Lord,
my spirit rejoices in God my savior.
For he noticed his handmaid's lowliness;
and from now on all will speak of me as blessed.
The Mighty One has done great things for me.
Holy is his name."

Reflection

Mary was truly desperate but trusted in God who provided her with everything she needed. Even though the manger wasn't exactly a five-star hotel, Mary and Joseph were able to bring Jesus into the world.

Like Mary, all of us are in some sense desperate and vulnerable. We are all in need of God's healing touch and presence in our lives. It is the experience of God's grace that prompts us to sing the greatness of God, and to rejoice.

Spiritual Exercise

For several days, we have focused on noticing the poor and desperate among us and doing our best to be God's hands and heart in our corner of the world. Today, peacefully contemplate the need or the ache that is in the deepest recesses of your heart.

God promises that if we serve as God's hands and heart in the world, we will be rewarded one-hundredfold. Offer the need of your heart to God and watch for the miracle of God's grace today. Remember, Advent is a time of waiting and patience, but if we share our anxiety and need with God while serving God in our neighbor, God will bring us more joy than we can imagine.

Praying with Jesus

Scripture Reading: Zephaniah 3:14–15

Sing joyfully, Israel!
Rejoice and exult with all your heart,
    daughter of Jerusalem.
The Lord has removed the judgment against
    you,
and has turned your enemies away.
The Lord is in your midst.
You will not experience evil again.

Reflection

Most of us suffer from the fact that there are people who simply do not seem to like us much. Sometimes, despite our best efforts, we have been labeled and cannot seem to move others to focus on our better selves. We are thought of perhaps as stingy, or crabby, or worse. We grieve because those who label us are often those with whom we would prefer to have good relations — family, friends, or colleagues. What a joy it would be if those who malign and misjudge us would stop their behavior, give us the benefit of the doubt, and choose to see the good in our soul.

Spiritual Exercise

When Jesus hung on the cross, judged and maligned, he prayed: "Father, forgive them, they do not know what they do." Today, think of those who misjudge you. Try ten times during the day to pray with Jesus, "Father, forgive them, they do not know what they do." If you feel that you have been part of the problem, include yourself in the "them" that needs to be forgiven.

Jesus' prayer on the cross eventually sent the Holy Spirit on Pentecost. Try to pray Jesus' prayer for those who hurt you until Christmas day, and watch for the Holy Spirit to break down barriers toward the legitimate respect that your soul deserves.

Surrendering to God

Scripture Reading: Psalm 23:6

Surely goodness and love will follow me
all the days of my life,
and I will dwell in the house of God
as long as I live.

Reflection

It is not that sheep do not experience evil in their world. The wolf prowls, the winter winds blow, colorful flowers that entice the eye may be poisonous. What brings peace to the sheep is the knowledge that the shepherd who protects them is navigating the dangers for them. The sheep are not in charge — the shepherd is.

Our world is full of many dangers that cause us anxiety and challenge our peace. Evil is a reality of our world. Those who are peaceful and joyful learn to understand that God is in charge and can even use evil for good if they simply place their fragile egos in God's hands.

Spiritual Exercise

When evil seemed to have the upper hand as Jesus hung on the cross, he prayed, "Father, into your hands I commend my spirit." Jesus had done all he could, but people still judged him as a blasphemer and insurrectionist. That these accusations and his ultimate fate came from the hands of those in charge of the religious identity he deeply loved was even more hurtful.

Today, admit to God those things that you suffer from but cannot control. Who misjudges you or causes you pain? Offer these situations to God at various times this day with the prayer of Jesus, "Father, into your hands I commend my spirit." As yesterday, continue this prayer with the prayer of forgiveness until Christmas day and expect that God's peace will transform the evil you experience into good in a way that, perhaps, you cannot imagine.

Light

four

1 Finding Our Home in God's Family

Scripture Reading: Romans 13:11–12

Do you know what time it is?
It is the hour for you to waken from your
   sleep,
for our salvation is nearer now than when
   we first accepted the faith.
The night is almost over,
and the day is at hand.
Let us, therefore, throw off the works of
   darkness
and put on the armor of life.

Reflection

Through Jesus, we are adopted as sons and daughters into the very Trinitarian life of God. To experience the integration of our human/divine existence, Jesus teaches us simple steps. We are to do what we can to live a moral life. We are to strip our lives of what is superfluous and avoid unnecessary anxieties. What we cannot change in our lives, we are to hand over to God, begging forgiveness for those who have hurt us and admitting that we are sometimes helpless to change the opinions and actions of others.

Now, at the end of our Advent preparation we hear, "Do you know what time it is? It is the hour for you to waken from your sleep, for our salvation is nearer now than when we first accepted the faith." It is time now to choose life and avoid temptations that undermine our human/divine dignity. It is time, now, for us to accept deeply the light of God's glory shining within us.

Spiritual Exercise

Today, imagine yourself living as a brother or sister within the dynamism of the family of God. In prayer today, address each person of the Trinitarian family and reflect about your relationship with God as Father/Mother, Jesus Christ, and the Holy Spirit.

2 Contemplating God's Glory

Scripture Reading: Philippians 3:20–21

Our citizenship is in heaven,
From there we eagerly await our savior,
    Jesus Christ.
His power will transform our lowly bodies
so that they will be like his glorious body.

Reflection

As Christians, we believe that both our soul and body live on after our death, but that our body is transformed into a glorious body, filled with the light of God.

We do not need to wait until death to become glorious. When Jesus came to earth as a baby, the shepherds were keeping watch of their sheep by night, and "the glory of the Lord shone around them." They were drawn by the glory of God to the manger where they saw for themselves the child Jesus. The kings were led by the glory of the star which also led them to the manger.

Spiritual Exercise:

Where do you experience the light or energy of God in your life? How might you try to multiply your God-given opportunities to allow the light of God to shine through you and reach others?

In prayer today, imagine yourself as a shepherd before Jesus in the manger. Allow the light of God's glory shining around and through the child Jesus to penetrate your soul. Silently sit, warmed by the light and energy of God's overflowing love.

3 Enlightening Our Judgments

Scripture Reading: 1 Corinthians 4:5

Therefore, do not judge your neighbor.
When the Lord comes,
he will bring to light what is hidden in
   darkness
and will manifest the motives of our hearts.
At that time, all will receive their praise from
   God.

Reflection

We know how hurtful it is to be judged or maligned by others. Most of us must admit that we, too, are guilty of judging others, of reducing their souls to disparaging caricatures. When we do this, we denigrate the creative genius of God expressed in unique ways through individual souls. Other people are not us. They think differently, act differently, even respond to God's voice in different ways. These differences express the creativity of God.

We are created in God's image. A judgmental spirit accuses God of making a mistake. God, we think, should have made all people in our own image. We, rather than God, become the standard by which we judge others. We demean the grandeur of God's creativity, and demand to judge others by our own narrow-minded standard.

Jesus came to earth as a small, poor baby. In humility, God came to earth not to judge but to redeem. We share in the glory, the light of the manger when we, too, stop judging our neighbor and humble ourselves before the grandeur of the glory of God's greatness.

Spiritual Exercise

Before Jesus as he lays in the manger, place all of your judgments of other people around the crib. Then, imagining the light of the star over the stable, ask God to enlighten your judgments of others.

4 Enjoying God's Light

Scripture Reading: Colossians 1:12–13

Let us give thanks to the Father for making
  us fit
to share in the inheritance of the saints in
  light.
God rescued us from the clutches of darkness
and brought us into the kingdom of his
  beloved Son.
In him we have redemption,
the forgiveness of our sins.

Reflection

Paul's message of good news is clear. It is God who makes us fit to share in the light of Christ's glory. We are not called to be perfect moral specimens, but we are asked to rely on God's grace and mercy that redeems us by forgiving our failings.

Although we were once in the darkness of anxiety, caused by thinking that we could re-deem ourselves, Christ brings us light if we do our part and hand the rest over to God. Rather than fret about our shortcomings, we are to give them back to God who transforms them into the very light of glory. For those of us who might have more than one shortcoming, this is very good news!

We do not live in God's light alone. Rather, as God's adopted sons and daughters, we are one with all the living, both in heaven and on earth, in praising God in the light of glory. Our very loneliness is transformed by God into a Trinitarian community of light and peace.

Spiritual Exercise

In the Middle Ages, Christians thought about light as being the very energy of God. They built Gothic churches with tall windows to let in as much sunlight as they could. Especially during the winter months, they wanted to know and experience the very light and warmth of God.

Do what you can today to appreciate the light in your world. Try to enjoy the sun — if you can find it — a little longer today. Spend time under the warmth of a lamp, or take the time to be enlightened by reading something that brings peace and harmony to your soul.

Contemplating Wisdom

Scripture Reading: Wisdom 7:26, 28–30

Wisdom is the refulgence of eternal light,
an untarnished mirror of God's activity,
and an image of God's goodness.
There is nothing God loves more than a
person
who abides with wisdom.

Reflection

While the ancients often worshipped the sun as a god, ancient Israelites honored the God of creation, experiencing the light of God as wisdom, the mirror of God's goodness.

When we meet a person who radiates light and peace, and is unburdened by superfluous anxieties, we know that we have met someone who is holy. We wish to be in that person's company, to share that person's wisdom, peace, and joy. We want to learn his or her secret.

Advent is a time for getting back to the very basics of welcoming an infant into the world, of finding our peace again, of handing over our worries and cares to God, and of discovering again the wisdom created and living within our very soul.

Spiritual Exercise

Think about a person you have encountered who you consider to be wise. Was he or she perfect? Free from shortcomings? If not, rest assured. You have evidence that God can truly abide among human creatures.

God wants us to trust that divine shepherding is enough. Look into your own soul a number of times today and again pray with Saint Clare: "I praise and thank you, God, for having created me!"

Pondering Our Christmas Family

Scripture Reading: Baruch 5:1–4

Take off your robe of sorrow and misery,
   Jerusalem,
and dress yourself forever in the beauty of
   God's glory.
Wrapped in the cloak of justice from God,
wear on your head the crown
that displays the glory of the Everlasting
   One.
God will show all the earth your splendor
and will give you evermore the name: "the
   peace of justice,"
and "the glory of God's adoration."
Rise up, Jerusalem.
Stand upon the height and look to the east.
See your children gathering from the east
   and west
rejoicing at the word of the Holy One.

Reflection

When we hand over to God our anxieties
and worries, and do our best to serve God in the
world, we become a person of wisdom — a lover

of God. When we are at peace with our own created reality, we exude the kind of wisdom that attracts the goodness of others.

In the hagiographical tradition, it is animals and children who best recognize the holy person. Still innocent, they seem to know instinctively those who have left behind anxiety and competiveness and have become what God created them to be. Even though wisdom is not always appreciated by those who still cling to anxiety, God's glory is loved by many. Sometimes, in order to have this glory appreciated, we need to spend more time with poor shepherds and lowly infants lying in mangers.

Spiritual Exercise

Examine who you are planning to spend Christmas with this year. Are these people who can appreciate simplicity and peace? Are there others whom you may wish to include in your Christmas celebrations that might be good company for you?

If so, invite those who might not expect your invitation and see what God creates. Perhaps you will find yourself with those "gathering from the east and west." If your holiday plans include a "peaceful bunch," reflect today on the blessing that God has given you and ask yourself how you might further share this blessing.

7 Christmas Day: Singing the Glory of God among Us

Scripture Reading: Isaiah 9:2; 6

The people who walked in darkness
have seen a great light.
They who once lived in gloom
now have light shining upon them.
A child is born to us!
He is called, "Wonderful," "Counselor,"
"Mighty God," "Eternal Father,"
and "Prince of Peace."

Reflection

Christians celebrate Jesus as the "child born to us" who is our light. Yet, the infant Jesus could do nothing by himself. He needed to be fed, clothed, and protected. As an infant, he was simply a child of God.

As we bring a close to this Advent season, we know that we are asked to offer God a moral and giving lifestyle. When we are challenged with our own shortcomings and character flaws, we are to hand these over to God who we trust will transform them into our glory.

Our call is not to be the light, but to be God's glory. We are to allow the light of God to shine through us without blocking this glory through anxiety and preoccupation. With Jesus, we are to be at peace with our helplessness and insignificance.

Spiritual Exercise

In your final preparations for Christmas, consider and be at peace with both your insignificance and glory as a child of God. Sing or play Christmas carols to begin your celebration of God's coming to dwell within our world and within the wonder of your own soul. Merry Christmas!

Also available in the same series:

Keepsakes for the Journey
Four Weeks on Faith Deepening
Susan Muto
ISBN: 978-1-56548-333-0, 72 pages

Pathways to Relationship
Four Weeks on Simplicity, Gentleness, Humility, Friendship
Robert F. Morneau
ISBN: 978-1-56548-317-0, 72 pages

Pathways to Community
Four Weeks on Prudence, Justice, Fortitude and Temperance
Robert F. Morneau
ISBN: 978-1-56548-303-3, 72 pages

Pathways to God
Four Weeks on Faith, Hope and Charity
Robert F. Morneau
ISBN: 978-1-56548-286-9, 72 pages

Peace of Heart
Reflections on Choices in Daily Life
Marc Foley
ISBN: 978-1-56548-293-7, 72 pages

Sister Earth
Creation, Ecology and the Spirit
Helder Camara
ISBN: 978-1-56548-299-9, 72 pages

Mother to All, Mother Forever
Four Weeks with Mary of Nazareth
Megan McKenna
ISBN: 978-1-56548-316-3, 72 pages

To order call 1-800-462-5980
or e-mail orders@newcitypress.com